What Can You See at the Bottom of the Sea?

Bottom of the Sea?

A Journey to the Mariana Trench Grade 5 | Children's Mystery & Wonders Books

BABY PROFESSOR
EDUCATION KIDS

First Edition, 2021

Published in the United States by Speedy Publishing LLC, 40 E Main Street, Newark, Delaware 19711 USA.

© 2021 Baby Professor Books, an imprint of Speedy Publishing LLC

Baby Professor Books are available at special discounts when purchased in bulk for industrial and sales-promotional use. For details contact our Special Sales Team at Speedy Publishing LLC, 40 E Main Street, Newark, Delaware 19711 USA. Telephone (888) 248-4521 Fax: (210) 519-4043.

10 9 8 7 6 * 5 4 3 2 1

Print Edition: 9781541954069
Digital Edition: 9781541957060
Hardcover Edition: 9781541984035

See the world in pictures. Build your knowledge in style.
www.speedypublishing.com

Table of Contents

SWIMMING IN THE OCEAN.

Have you ever gone swimming in an ocean? If not, have you ever been aboard a boat? Do you have any idea what the bottom of the ocean looks like? People used to assume that the bottom of the ocean was flat. That is not the case at all!

This book will describe what the bottom of the ocean looks like. It will also identify and talk about different types of mountains. It will even guide you through an activity in which you can make one mountain type for yourself.

THE BOTTOM OF THE OCEAN IS NOT FLAT AT ALL!

Chapter One:
The Ocean

The surface of the Earth sits on top of several plates. These plates float above molten rock. This area of molten rock is called the mantle. The plates are known as tectonic plates. When these plates converge, which is to push up against each other, we can get mountains. Plate movements can also create flat land when they move away, which is to diverge. These plates are why the ocean floor is not always completely smooth.

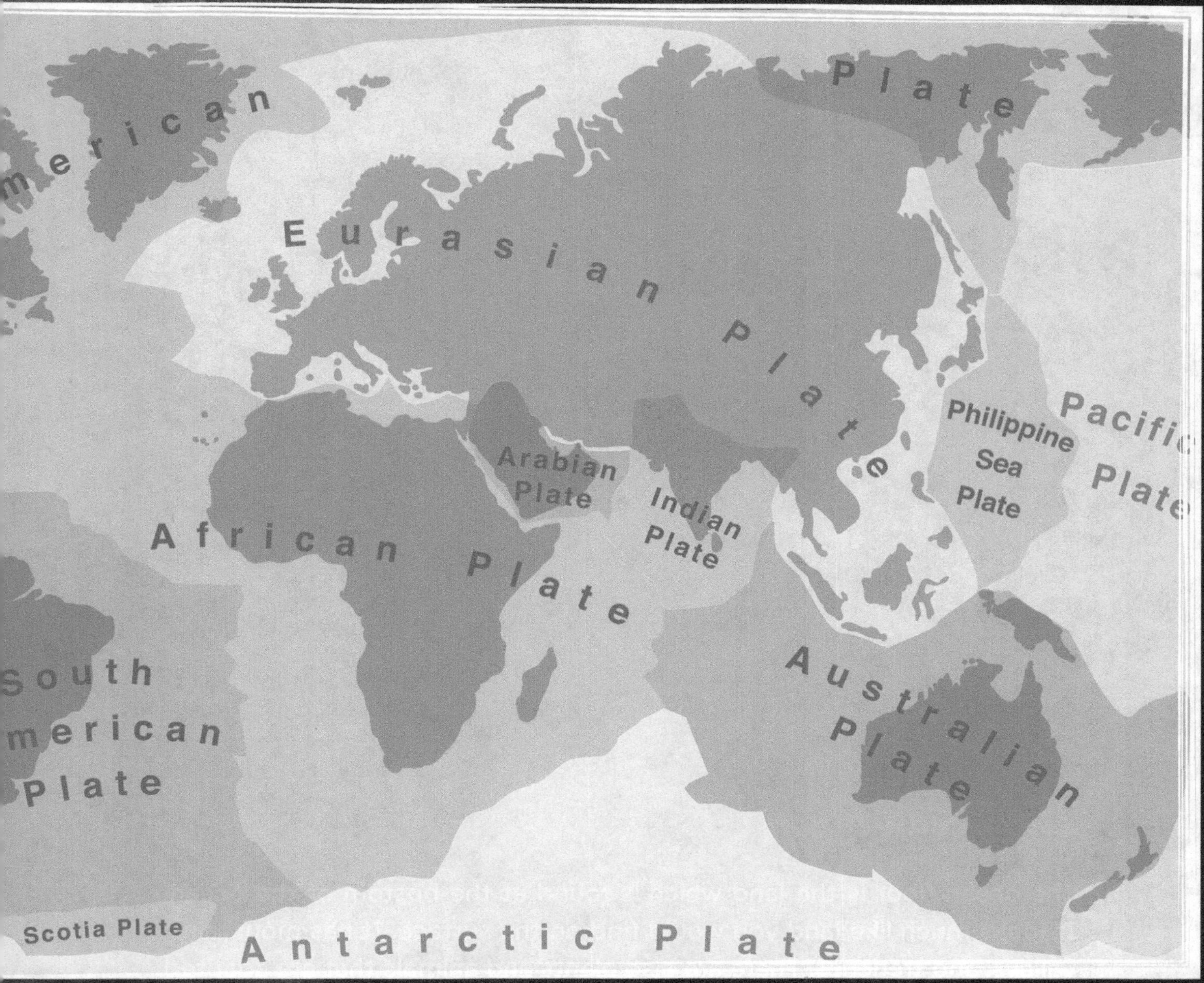
merican
Plate
Eurasian Plate
Pacific Plate
Philippine Sea Plate
Arabian Plate
Indian Plate
African Plate
South merican Plate
Australian Plate
Scotia Plate
Antarctic Plate

THE OCEAN FLOOR IS THE LAND WHICH IS FOUND AT THE BOTTOM OF THE OCEAN.

The Ocean Floor:

The ocean floor is the land which is found at the bottom of the ocean. It looks much like land you would find on the surface. It has mountains, valleys, and trenches. There are also plants and animals that are adapted to living underwater there.

NATURAL TRENCH INTO THE CORAL REEF CARVED BY WAVE SWELL.

THE OCEAN FLOOR HAS PLANTS AND ANIMALS THAT ARE ADAPTED TO LIVING UNDERWATER.

PLATE BOUNDARIES

DIVERGENT PLATE BOUNDARY

CONVERGENT PLATE BOUNDARY

TRANSFORM PLATE BOUNDARY

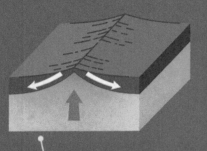
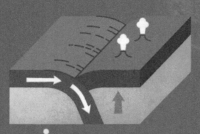

Oceanic Ridge

Oceanic Trench

Transform Fault

OCEAN

CRUST

MANTLE

THE MEETING POINT OF THE EDGES OF TWO PLATES IS CALLED A PLATE BOUNDARY.

There is a tectonic plate at the bottom of the Pacific Ocean. It is called the Pacific Plate. There are several other tectonic plates that meet up at the edges of the Pacific Plate. The meeting point of the edges of two plates is called a plate boundary.

Ocean Basins:

When plates move away from each other the molten rock will rise to fill the space. The molten rock under the crust is called magma. As the magma cools, it becomes new land.

WHEN PLATES MOVE AWAY FROM EACH OTHER THE MOLTEN ROCK WILL RISE TO FILL THE SPACE.

OCEANIC BASIN

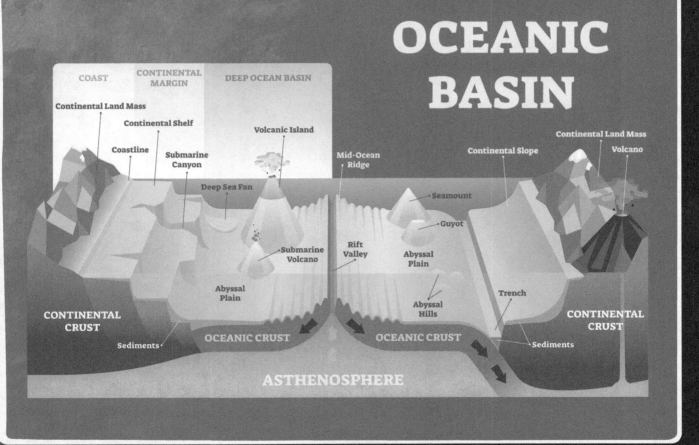

COAST

CONTINENTAL MARGIN

DEEP OCEAN BASIN

Continental Land Mass

Continental Shelf

Coastline

Submarine Canyon

Deep Sea Fan

Volcanic Island

Mid-Ocean Ridge

Continental Slope

Continental Land Mass

Volcano

Seamount

Guyot

Submarine Volcano

Rift Valley

Abyssal Plain

Abyssal Plain

Trench

Abyssal Hills

CONTINENTAL CRUST

Sediments

OCEANIC CRUST

OCEANIC CRUST

Sediments

CONTINENTAL CRUST

ASTHENOSPHERE

OCEAN BASINS

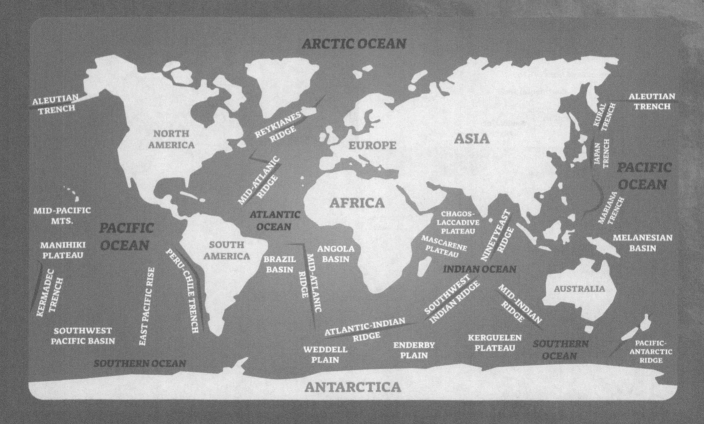

ILLUSTRATION OF THE OCEAN BASINS OF THE WORLD.

These new regions of land are typically lower than the surrounding regions. This will cause water to rush in to fill the area resulting in an ocean basin. Ocean basins can form under the ocean, or if the lower area is near the ocean.

Between Africa and Asia there is the Red Sea. This is an example of a growing area of water. The two continents are diverging. This is leading to the creation of new segments of the ocean floor. The Red Sea covers the surface of this new land causing its area to grow.

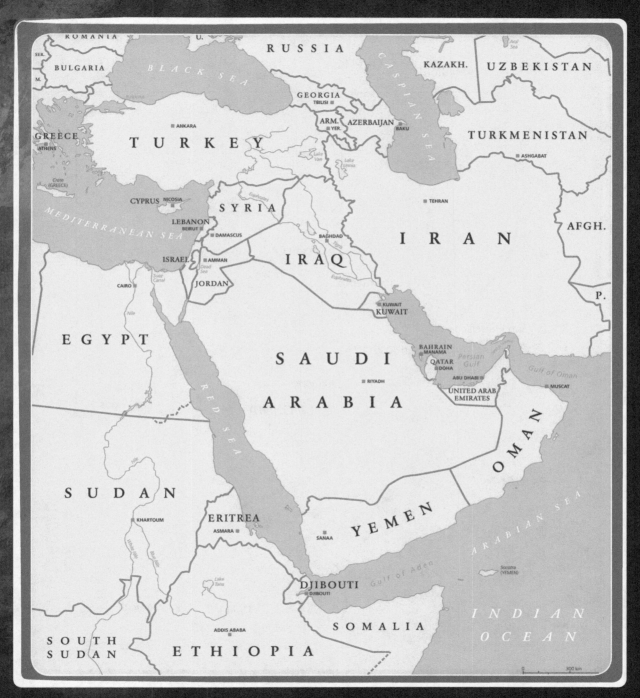

THE RED SEA IS FOUND BETWEEN AFRICA AND ASIA.

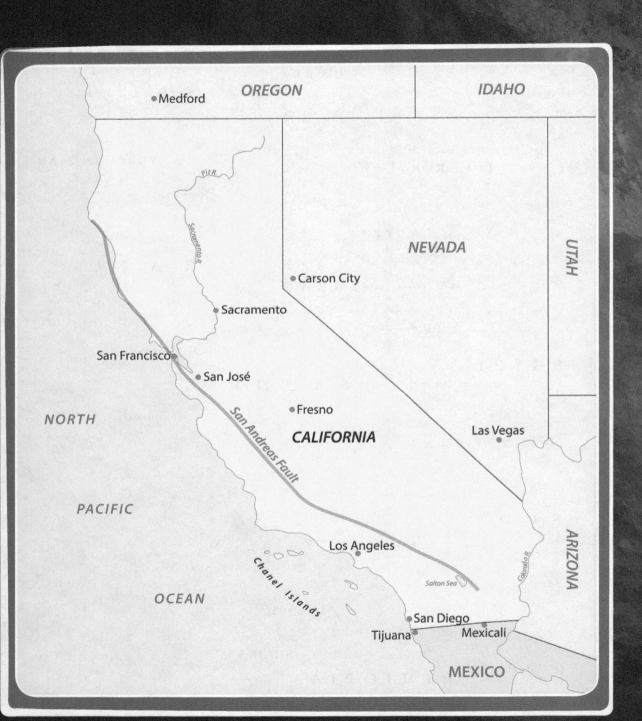

A fault is a large crack in the crust. In the United States, there is a fault called the San Andreas fault. It runs through Southern California to Northern Mexico. What this means is that Baja California is being increasingly separated from Mexico proper. As more and more ocean floor grows, the further they will diverge.

A VIEW OF THE SAN ANDREAS FAULT FROM JOSHUA TREE NATIONAL PARK.

Trenches:

Another way for tectonic plates to interact is through subduction. Subduction is a type of convergence. Instead of resulting in mountains being formed, subduction is when at least one plate is forced down into the mantle. Subduction can result in large trenches. Places where trenches are common are typically near subduction zones.

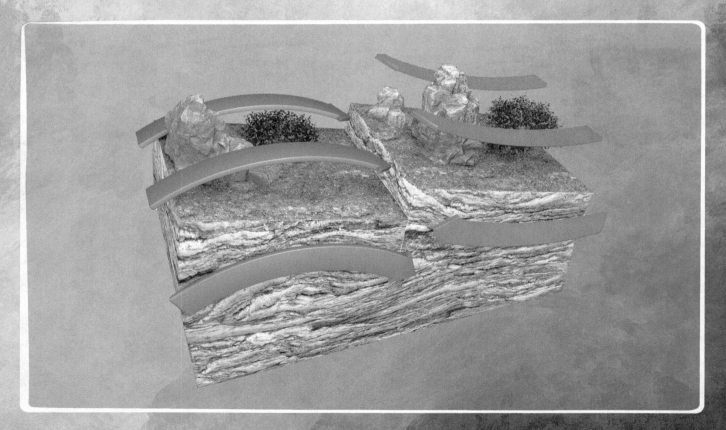

SUBDUCTION IS WHEN AT LEAST ONE PLATE IS FORCED DOWN INTO THE MANTLE.

SUBDUCTION CAN RESULT IN LARGE TRENCHES.

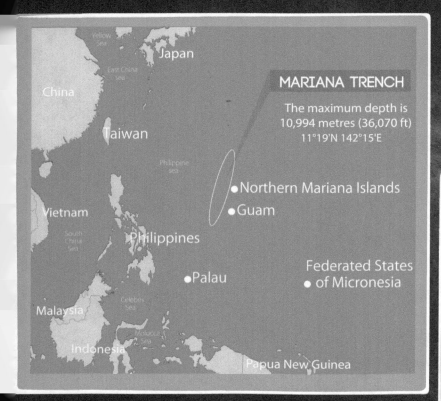

MARIANA TRENCH

The maximum depth is
10,994 metres (36,070 ft)
11°19'N 142°15'E

● Northern Mariana Islands
● Guam

Federated States
● of Micronesia

● Palau

THE MARIANA TRENCH IS FOUND
NEAR THE COAST OF GUAM.

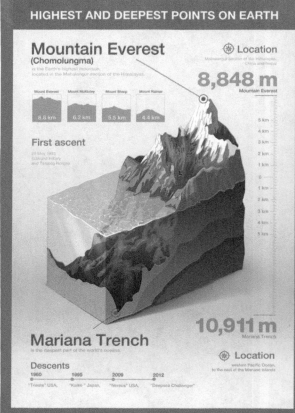

THE ENTIRETY OF MOUNT EVEREST
COULD FIT IN THE MARIANA TRENCH
WITH OVER A MILE TO SPARE!

THE MARIANA TRENCH IS THE DEEPEST PLACE ON EARTH.

The deepest place on Earth is a trench under the Pacific Ocean. It is called the Mariana Trench. It is found near the coast of Guam. The trench is 36,201 feet deep. The plate that was forced below into the mantle lies at a 40-degree angle to the other plate it collided with. The entirety of Mount Everest could fit in the Mariana Trench with over a mile to spare! (Mount Everest is the tallest mountain on our planet!)

Humans have made it to the bottom of the Mariana Trench. Two men from the U.S. Navy were able to take a bathyscape down to the bottom. A bathyscape is a special vessel that can be used to navigate underwater. It can go deeper than a submarine.

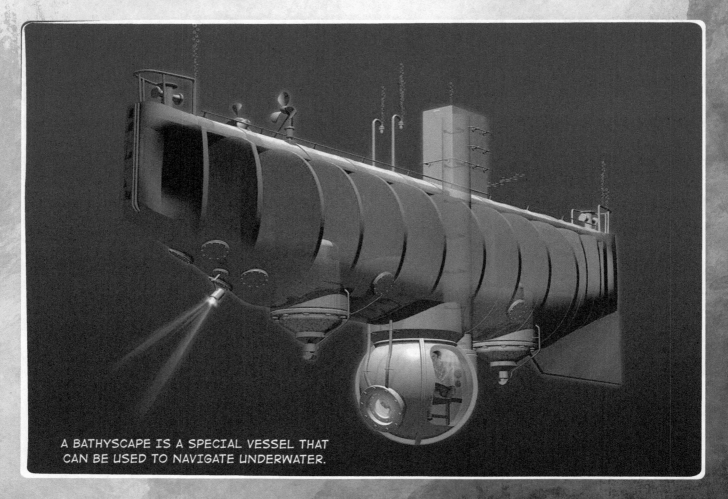

A BATHYSCAPE IS A SPECIAL VESSEL THAT CAN BE USED TO NAVIGATE UNDERWATER.

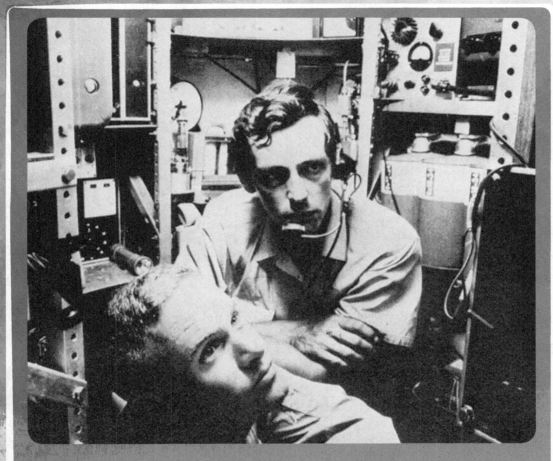

JACQUES PICCARD AND DON WALSH INSIDE *TRIESTE*, A DEEP-SEA SUBMERSIBLE, WHICH THEY USED TO DESCEND TO THE DEEPEST KNOWN PART IN THE MARIANA TRENCH – THE CHALLENGER DEEP.

Humans need special equipment to go down so low. We need oxygen to breathe. We also need to be able to survive the immense pressure of so much water crushing us.

Volcanoes, Earthquakes, and Mountains:

The opposite of trench formation would be the formation of mountains. Instead of plates being pushed downwards, they are pushed upwards. There is a chain of mountains underwater called the mid-Ocean ridge. They were formed in this manner.

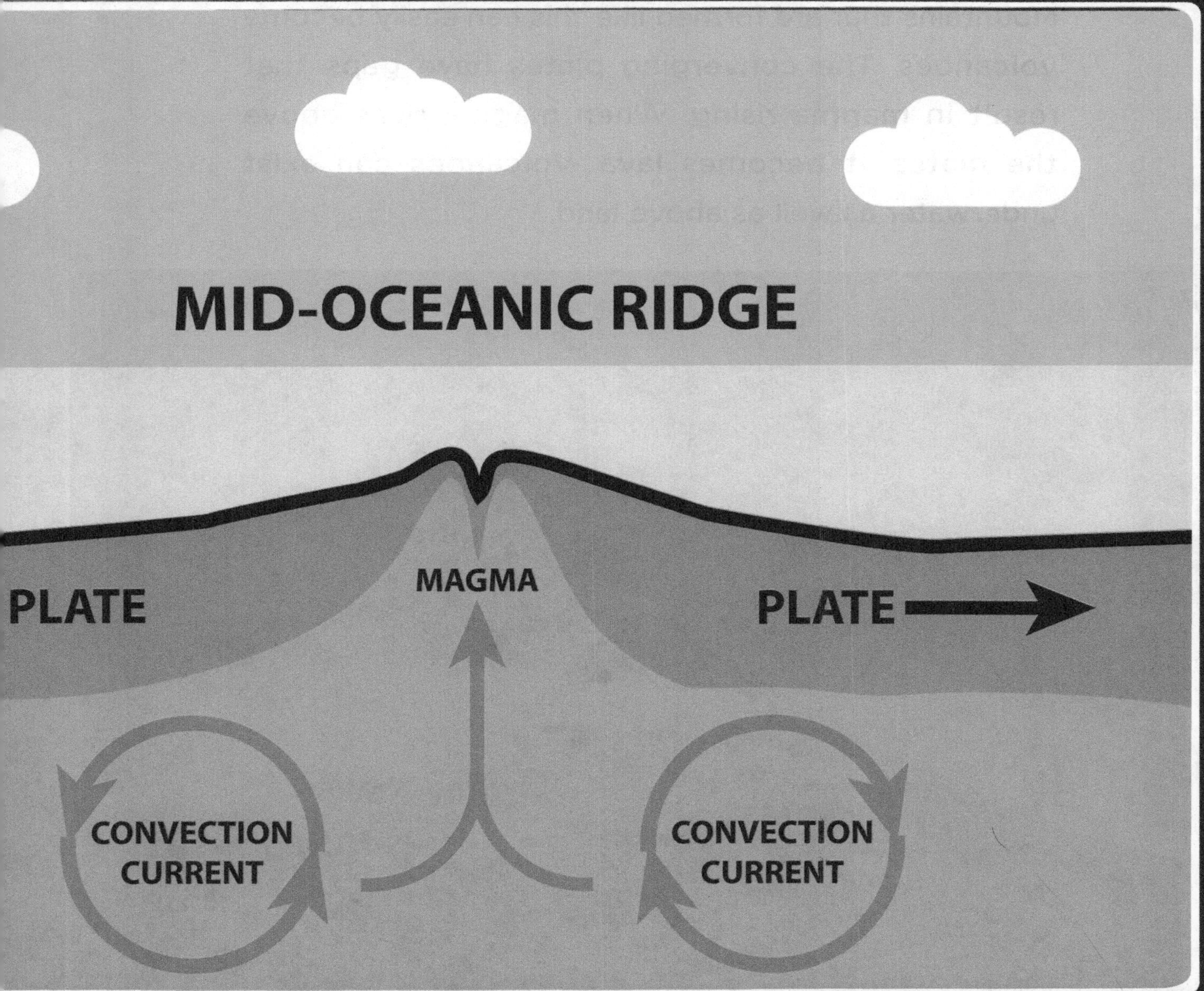

MID-OCEANIC RIDGE

PLATE

MAGMA

PLATE →

CONVECTION CURRENT

CONVECTION CURRENT

THE MID-OCEANIC RIDGE IS A CHAIN OF MOUNTAINS FOUND UNDERWATER.

Mountains that are formed like this can easily become volcanoes. The converging plates have gaps that result in magma rising. When magma rises above the plates, it becomes lava. Volcanoes can exist underwater as well as above land.

MAYON VOLCANO IS AN ACTIVE STRATOVOLCANO IN THE ISLAND OF LUZON IN THE PHILIPPINES.

THE ISLET OF VILA FRANCA DO CAMPO AZORES, PORTUGAL, IS
FORMED BY THE CRATER OF AN OLD UNDERWATER VOLCANO.

EARTHQUAKES ARE CAUSED BY THE RUBBING TOGETHER OF PLATES.

Earthquakes and volcanoes often go hand in hand. Earthquakes are caused by the rubbing together of plates. When enough pressure is created, the shockwaves can move outward making the crust shake.

EARTHQUAKES
Types of plate boundary

Normal fault

Reverse fault

Left-lateral strike
Slip fault

Right-lateral strike
Slip fault

Chapter Two:
Different Mountains

VESTRAHORN MOUNTAIN ON STOKKSNES CAPE IN ICELAND.

ountains are formed along the boundaries of tectonic plates. They are formed in different ways. Some mountains are not even made directly by plates colliding. Instead, they are formed from the magma that can be released. This chapter will teach you about dome-shaped mountains, folded mountains, fault block mountains, and volcanic mountains.

Dome-shaped Mountains:

Dome-shaped mountains happen when magma is forced upwards. The bulge can result in a mountain that is shaped like a dome. Sometimes the pressure will build until the magma finally erupts and a new volcano is formed. Other times, the magma will slowly cool into granite rock. The bulge remains behind as a mountain.

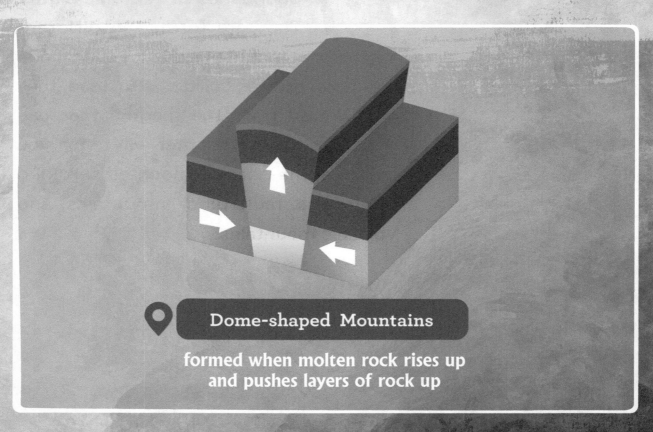

Dome-shaped Mountains

formed when molten rock rises up
and pushes layers of rock up

A SNOW CAPPED DOME-SHAPED MOUNTAIN RISING OUT OF WATERSIDE
EVERGREENS IN THE ALASKAN WILDERNESS.

GRANITE ROCK FORMATIONS IN THE BLACK HILLS OF SOUTH DAKOTA.

Over time, the crust that surrounded the granite may erode. Erosion is when rock gets chipped away over time by different forces of weather. The result is a granite mountain. An example of these granite mountains can be seen in the Black Hills of South Dakota.

Folded Mountains

formed when converging plates push upwards

Folded Mountains:

Folded Mountains are the more basic idea of mountains. They are caused when converging plates push upwards. Picture laying a paper towel flat on the counter. Lay your palms down on either side of the towel and push inwards. The towel should fold upwards. The same thing happens when the movement of tectonic plates results in folded mountains.

FOLDED MOUNTAINS ARE CAUSED WHEN CONVERGING PLATES PUSH UPWARDS.

MT. EVEREST WAS CREATED THROUGH CONVERGING PLATES AND
IT CAN BE CLASSIFIED AS A FOLD MOUNTAIN.

The tallest mountain on Earth, Mt. Everest, is over 29,000 feet. It is a part of a range of mountains called the Himalayas. This mountain range is in Asia. Mt. Everest was created through converging plates and it can be classified as a fold mountain.

It is thought that the plate that India, a country in Asia, is on hit the Asian tectonic plate. This resulted in the plates being pushed upwards and forced to rise from the ocean.

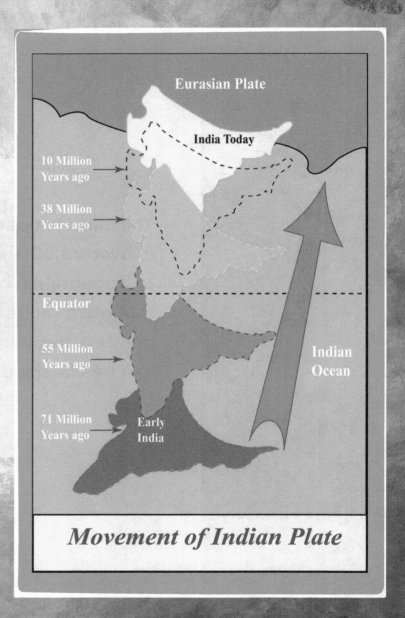

Eurasian Plate

India Today

10 Million Years ago

38 Million Years ago

Equator

55 Million Years ago

Indian Ocean

71 Million Years ago

Early India

Movement of Indian Plate

IT IS THOUGHT THAT THE PLATE THAT INDIA IS ON HIT THE ASIAN TECTONIC PLATE.

Since fossils of sea creatures have been found high up in the Himalayas, the land must have been underwater at some point.

FOSSILS OF PRIMORDIAL AQUATIC LIFE AMMONITE FOUND IN
LANGZA IN SPITI VALLEY, HIMACHAL PRADESH, INDIA.

Volcanic Mountains:

Volcanic mountains are mountains that have had volcanic eruptions. The eruptions happen when enough magma builds up to get spewed out. As the magma leaves the mantle, it cools on the surface of the Earth. It will then harden. The ash that is released also falls on the mountain sides. It too hardens. The result is a mountain that grows. The more lava that flows, the more eruptions, the larger the mountain gets.

CHIMBORAZO IS THE HIGHEST VOLCANO AND MOUNTAIN IN ECUADOR.

MT. ST. HELENS IN SKAMANIA COUNTY, WASHINGTON.

Volcanic eruptions can occur from mountains that already have some size. They can also come from tiny vents that explode. Over time, the building up of hardened lava results in cone shaped mountains. Mt. St. Helens is an example of a volcanic mountain.

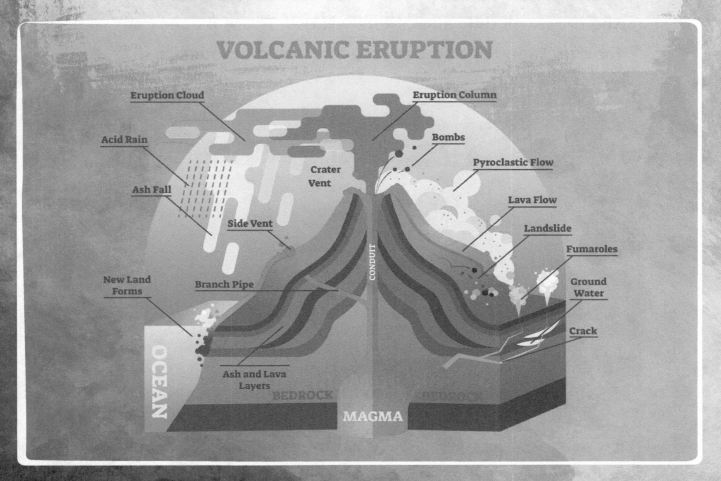

VOLCANIC ERUPTIONS CAN OCCUR FROM MOUNTAINS THAT ALREADY HAVE SOME SIZE.

Fault-Block Mountains:

We learned in the first chapter that faults are cracks in the surface of the Earth. They are caused by the plates moving. Sometimes when these cracks form, parts of the crust will sink, and others will rise. These pieces can look rectangular and become fault-block mountains.

Fault-Block Mountains

formed when a block of rock drops lower than other blocks

THE HARZ MOUNTAINS IN GERMANY ARE EXAMPLES OF FAULT-BLOCK MOUNTAINS.

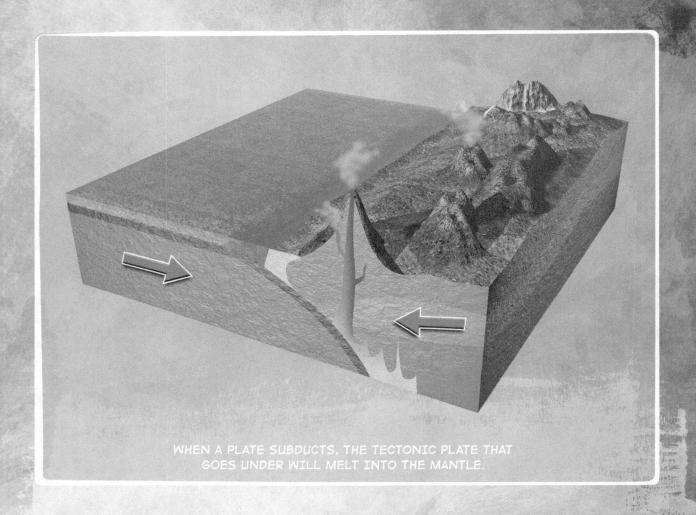

WHEN A PLATE SUBDUCTS, THE TECTONIC PLATE THAT
GOES UNDER WILL MELT INTO THE MANTLE.

There are some added ways pressure can be created to cause these faults. In addition, it will cause the rise and fall of land. When a plate subducts, the tectonic plate that goes under will melt into the mantle.

In some cases, magma that rises during this process will cool as granite. The granite will force the plate to rise. This will result in some pressure. Granite is known to be quite hard. It is often used in the construction of countertops.

MASSIVE GRANITE ROCK IN
YOSEMITE NATIONAL PARK.

GRANITE IS OFTEN USED IN THE
CONSTRUCTION OF COUNTERTOPS.

When large blocks of granite are pressed against a fault, increasing the rise and fall of land in such areas, we can get mountains and mountain ranges. These kinds of mountains are called fault-block mountains. These granite mountains are not the same as dome mountains.

TETON RANGE IN WYOMING IS AN EXAMPLE OF FAULT-BLOCK MOUNTAINS.

The Sierra Nevada Mountains were formed in this fashion. Subduction began over one hundred million years ago. The Pacific Plate was forced under the North American Plate. The subduction resulted in magma slowly cooling into mammoth granite blocks.

These granite giants placed pressure on the Sierra fault. Once this happened, mountains were made. They are the Sierra Nevada Mountains that we can see in California.

SIERRA NEVADA MOUNTAINS

GEOLOGISTS THINK THAT THE SIERRA NEVADA MOUNTAINS ARE STILL BEING FORMED.

The rising granite also created pressure. This pressure cracked the eastern side of the mountain range. This resulted in the Sierra Nevada fault line. Earthquakes still occur in this area. Geologists, people who study all about the ground of the Earth, think that the Sierra Nevada mountains are still being formed. Geologists have measured remarkable growth of the mountains in that range.

An Activity to Make a Fault-Block Mountain:

To get an idea of how fault-block mountains might form, we can do a simple activity. It is outlined below.

Materials:

You will need two sponges that are the same size, a stiff piece of cardboard, a pencil, a pair of scissors and some tape. You should ask a parent or guardian to supervise.

SPONGES

PIECE OF CARDBOARD

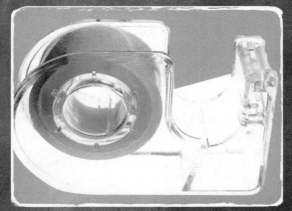

TAPE

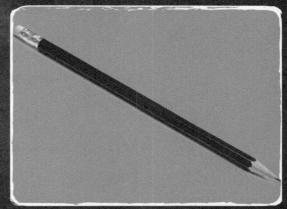

PENCIL

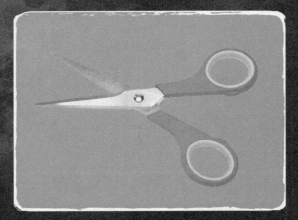

PAIR OF SCISSORS

TRACE THE SHAPE OF THE SPONGE ONTO THE CARDBOARD AND CUT THE SHAPE OUT.

Procedure:

Trace the shape of the sponge onto the cardboard. Cut the shape out and tape it to the bottom of one of the sponges. Ideally, the cardboard and the sponge will be the same size. Next, place the two sponges next to each other so that the ends touch. Now try to force the two sponges together. What do you think will happen?

Imagine that these sponges are tectonic plates. One of the plates, the one with the cardboard, is heavier than the other one. You should observe that the heavier sponge will be forced downward.

AN ILLUSTRATION SHOWING THE GEOLOGICAL PROCESSES THAT OCCUR AT A SUBDUCTION ZONE BETWEEN TWO TECTONIC PLATES.

This mimics subduction. What happens is that, as one plate moves downwards, it forces the other upward. It has also provided some support. We have the beginning of a new mountain.

At the very bottom of the ocean lies the ocean floor. Instead of being flat, it is made up of different formations. It contains trenches, basins, mountains and even volcanoes! Mountains that are on the surface of the Earth come in different forms. The form that a mountain will take is influenced by the activity that made it a mountain in the first place. This book described the ocean floor and mountain formations. For exciting facts about what makes up other parts of the Earth, including its atmosphere, look for other Baby Professor books!

Made in the USA
Coppell, TX
26 January 2024